Dear Family,

What's the best way to help your child love reading?

Find good books like this one to share—and read together!

Here are some tips.

●**Take a "picture walk."** Look at all the pictures before you read. Talk about what you see.

●**Take turns.** Read to your child. Ham it up! Use different voices for different characters, and read with feeling! Then listen as your child reads to you, or explains the story in his or her own words.

●**Point out words as you read.** Help your child notice how letters and sounds go together. Point out unusual or difficult words that your child might not know. Talk about those words and what they mean.

●**Ask questions.** Stop to ask questions as you read. For example: "What do you think will happen next?" "How would you feel if that happened to you?"

●**Read every day.** Good stories are worth reading more than once! Read signs, labels, and even cereal boxes with your child. Visit the library to take out more books. And look for other JUST FOR YOU! BOOKS you and your child can share!

The Editors

Courtland Wilson Branch Library
303 Washington Ave.
New Haven, CT 06519-1801

For Stephen in England,
and all the wonderful Sundays there.
—JGF

To Danny and Stepfon
—CB

Text copyright © 2003 by Juwanda G. Ford-Williams.
Illustrations copyright © 2003 by Colin Bootman.
Produced for Scholastic by COLOR-BRIDGE BOOKS, LLC, Brooklyn, NY
All rights reserved. Published by SCHOLASTIC INC.
JUST FOR YOU! is a trademark of Scholastic Inc.

No part of this publication may be reproduced in whole or in part, or stored in a retrieval system, or transmitted in any form or by any means, electronic, mechanical, photocopying, recording, or otherwise, without written permission of the publisher. For information regarding permission, write to Scholastic Inc., 557 Broadway, New York, NY 10012.

ISBN 0-439-56854-4

Library of Congress Cataloging-in-Publication Data is available.

10 9 8 7 6 5 4 3 2

03 04 05 06 07

Printed in the U.S.A.

23

First Scholastic Printing, November 2003

Sunday Best

by Juwanda G. Ford
Illustrated by Colin Bootman

JUST FOR YOU! Level 3

Monday through Friday, we do almost the same thing every day. Early in the morning, Mom leaves for work. Then Dad takes my sister and me to school.

FORD
Ford, Juwanda G.
Sunday best
Courtland Wilson Branch Library
303 Washington Ave.
New Haven, CT 06519-1601
35000093568847 Children's

READER
FORD

Late in the afternoon, Dad hurries
off to his job. Mom rushes home. She
makes sure we let her know if we have
any homework.

I like something about every day
of the week. I like pizza on Monday.
My school has really good pizza!

I like piano lessons
on Tuesday.

I like taking out the trash
on Wednesday.

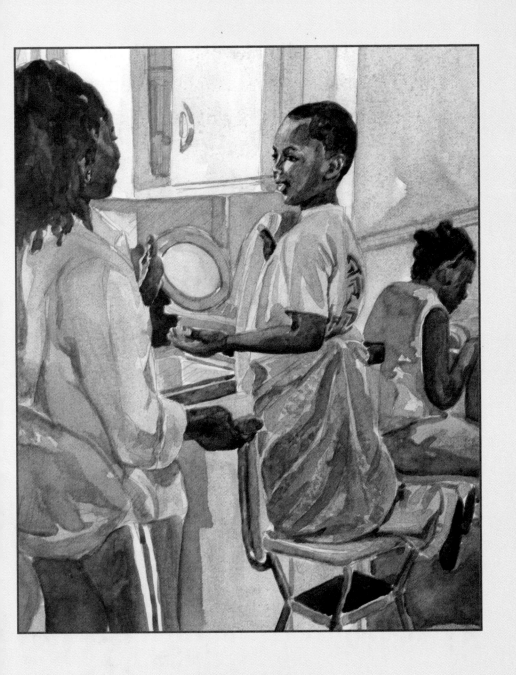

I even like doing the dishes
on Thursday!

And I really like fish-fry Friday. Mom makes fish taste even better than pizza. That's why my friends come over for dinner.

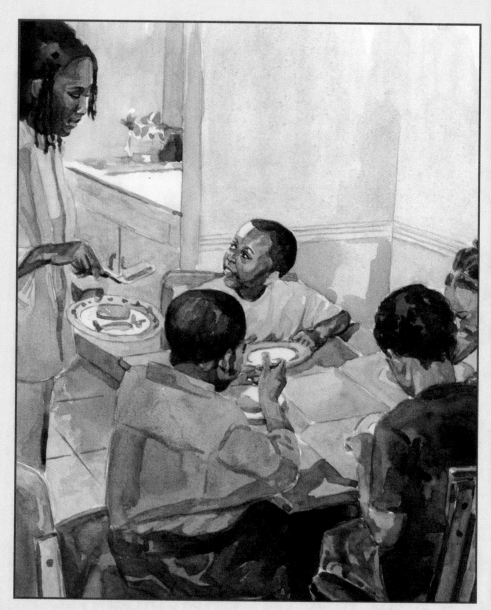

On Saturdays, things are a little
different. Saturday mornings, Mom and I
take karate lessons. I love karate!

Dad and my sister go shopping. Then
my sister and I put away the groceries.

Later we all have chores to do.

But Sundays are really different.
On Sundays, we do everything best!

We eat our biggest and best breakfast of the week.

We put on our best clothes—
our Sunday best.
Dad and I both wear ties.

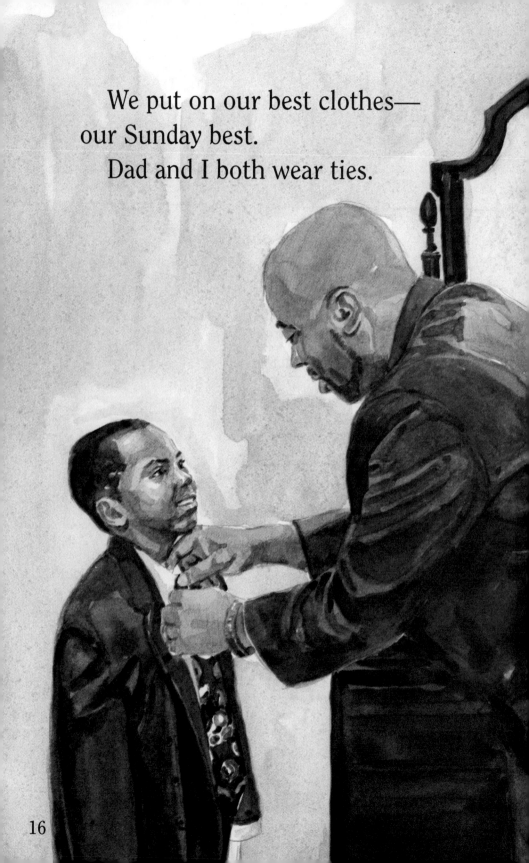

On the way to service, we walk our best Sunday walk. We don't walk our "we're in a hurry, don't want to be late" walk.

We stroll through the park. We stop to say hello to friends, or watch the bike riders, or look at the flowers.

During service, my sister and I are on our best behavior. We try not to talk—and if we talk, we whisper.

Until it's time to sing. Then we
get loud! We sing and clap as loudly as
we can.

Some Sundays we visit Grandma and Grandpa. My aunt and uncle and Cousin Squeaky come, too.

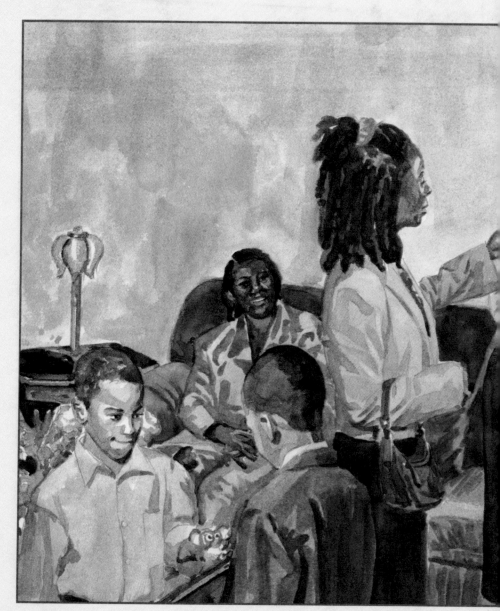

Squeaky is not just my
cousin. He's my best friend.

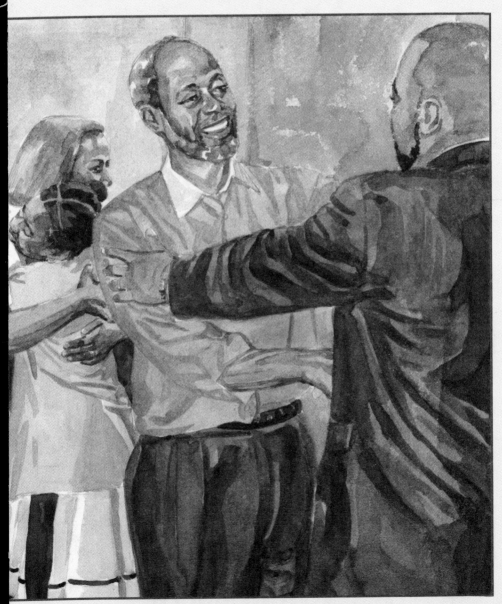

Sometimes everyone comes over
to visit us.

Dad lights up the grill and makes his famous Sunday-best barbecue.

But most Sundays, we go
home after service and relax.

We read the paper together. I help Mom clip out the coupons. Dad does the crossword puzzle. My sister reads the comics to us. We laugh and laugh!

Mom says that Sunday is
family day. It's true!

No matter what we do on Sunday, the four of us do it together, all day long. That's why I like Sunday best!

Here are some fun things for you to do.

The BEST Words Are YOURS!

The boy in this story has a very busy life! Go back to the beginning of the story on page 4. Turn each page. Use the pictures as clues to tell about his week again—in YOUR words!

Wonderful Words

▲ This story is loaded with words. Look for your favorites. Tell why you like them. Make a list of YOUR wonderful words.

▲ Are there any words that are new to you? Are there any that are hard to read? How about *pizza, piano, karate, groceries, behavior, coupons?* Find them in the story. Think about what they mean.

YOUR Best and Worst!

The boy likes Sunday
best of all.
Which day of the week is
YOUR favorite?
Which day is your
least favorite?
Talk about why that day
is the worst!

▲▲▲▲ TOGETHER TIME ▲▲▲▲

Make some time to share ideas about the story with your young reader! Here are some activities you can try. There are no right or wrong answers.

Read It Again: Invite your child to read the story aloud, with feeling! Talk about how the boy would sound when he talks about the things he likes best.

Act It Out: What does the boy mean when he talks about the "we're in a hurry, don't want to be late" walk? What does that kind of walk look like? Take turns acting out a hurried walk. Talk about how a *stroll* is different. Pretend to take a stroll through the park. Don't forget to wave to the friends you meet!

Read More: Read page 32 together to find out more about the author and artist. How are they like the characters in this book? Do they look the way you thought they would? You can visit the library to find other books by them.

Meet the Author

JUWANDA G. FORD says, "My grandmother raised my sister and me. Sundays were always special for us. She would sprinkle us with sweet-smelling powder and dress us in our best clothes. Then we would walk to church. Afterwards, Grandma would cook a big dinner with finger-licking fried chicken. During the summer she would put the chicken in a basket and take us to the park. We would play and splash in the children's sprinkler there for hours. Sunday was—and still is—my favorite day of the week."

Juwanda was born and raised in New Orleans, Louisiana. She went to college in Texas and in Oxford, England. She has worked for several children's book publishers in New York City. She lives with her husband in Brooklyn, New York, and is a full-time writer.

Meet the Artist

COLIN BOOTMAN says, "When I was young, Sunday was a big day for me! Every Sunday my family would get up and go to church. Then we would go visit family members we hadn't seen for a while—a lot like the family in this story. Painting the pictures for this book brought back so many good memories. And the park in the story is just like a park near my apartment building."

Colin was born in Trinidad in the West Indies and moved to the United States when he was seven years old. He studied art at the School of Visual Arts in New York City. He has illustrated many books for children, including *In My Momma's Kitchen* by Jerdine Nolen, and *Don't Say Ain't* by Irene Smalls. Colin lives with his family in Brooklyn, New York.